Cake Decorating

igloobooks

Published in 2015
by Igloo Books Ltd
Cottage Farm
Sywell
NN6 0BJ
www.igloobooks.com

Food photography and recipe development: PhotoCuisine UK
Front and back cover images © PhotoCuisine UK

HON005 0215
2 4 6 8 10 9 7 5 3 1
ISBN 978-1-78440-406-2

Printed and manufactured in China

Contents

Cake Decorating

Cook's Basics

  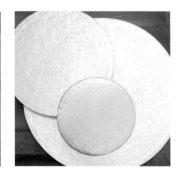

Tools and Equipment

While some cakes are very simple to decorate and require very little specialist equipment, there are others that will require you to have some more specialist tools to hand.

Icing cutters: cutters come in many different shapes and sizes, from simple circular cutters to novelty shapes and push-out cutters that also pattern the icing. They are available in most cook shops and supermarkets, but for more specialist equipment you may have to look online or in specialist cake decorating shops.

Cutters enable you to make much more precise shapes for decorating your cakes and it's worth investing in a range of different sizes and shapes and building up a collection over time.

Cake boards: cake boards provide a stable, hygienic base for your cakes and come in a variety of sizes and thicknesses. Generally, you'll need cake boards that are about 2 cm (1 in) wider than the base of your cake. If you are also decorating the boards with icing and novelties, you will need cake boards with a larger diameter.

Marble slab and chocolate tools: making delicate chocolate decorations, such as curls, requires a clean and even work surface that remains cool, such as a marble slab. For chocolate work, have clean sharp tools at the ready. A new wallpaper scraper and palette knives will enable you to more easily make chocolate curls and cigarillos.

Greaseproof paper / baking parchment: these are used for lining cake tins, making piping bags and providing a non-stick surface to work sugarcraft on.

Sugarcraft tools: specialist shops sell a wide range of tools designed specifically for decorating cakes. These include moulds for fondant, border cutters, crimpers and modelling tools, including:

Bone tool: ideal for thinning and smoothing the edges of leaves, flower petals and frills.

Serrated and tapered cone tool: used to indent paste to create a cone-shaped hollow, ideal for modelling marzipan fruits such as apples. The serrated cone is good for creating detailed and realistic throats of flowers.

Scriber tool: used for transcribing designs onto sugar plaques or cake sides, royal icing, sugarpaste or chocolate. The scriber tool is most useful for marking outlines of designs that you intend to pipe or paint onto a cake.

Ball tool: a great tool to cup and shape leaves, petals and frills. The small end is ideal for creating detail on marzipan figures.

Foam modelling mats: these enable the cake decorator to easily and hygienically work with sugarpaste. The mat acts as a soft base to model delicate elements of sugarcraft and also acts as a useful place to allow sugarcraft shapes to harden.

Heat lamps and latex gloves: when working with pulled sugar, you'll need to have a high-powered heat lamp to keep the sugar malleable and a large box of latex gloves to provide hygienic protection from the heat of the sugar.

Cake polishers and rolling pins: in order to get a professional finish to your icing work, you'll need cake polishers to smooth out uneven blemishes in your fondant icing, as well as to prepare flat, even surfaces in your fondant icing. Rolling pins of different sizes will enable you to work with larger and smaller pieces of fondant, to create uniform thicknesses.

Food dye and paintbrushes: there are many different types and shades of food dyes using both natural and artificial ingredients. Liquid, gel and dry powder dyes are available and enable the cake decorator to dye soft and hard fondants, cakes and sugar.

A clean set of paintbrushes are essential for the cake decorator and can be used for painting directly onto icing, sticking decorations to cakes and manipulating and giving texture to sugarpaste. Always wash and dry your brushes thoroughly to prevent them from clogging.

Cake tins: cake tins are another essential for the baker and cake decorator and it's worth investing in a set of heavy-bottomed cake tins of different sizes and shapes to enable you to create a wide variety of cakes.

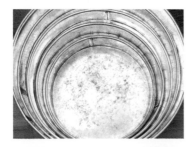

Piping bags and nozzles: these are a sugarcraft staple and the cake decorator should have a good selection of piping bags and nozzles to enable them to pipe different effects and different icings onto cakes.

Kitchen thermometer: for high heat sugar work, such as spinning sugar and pulling sugar, it's essential that you have a kitchen thermometer to measure the temperature of your mixtures to ensure that the techniques work properly.

Pump action sugarpaste gun: used to create a variety of fondant effects, where the consistency of the icing is too thick for standard piping. The guns come with a variety of apertures to create a huge range of fondant effects, including different shaped fondant ropes, hair and scallops.

Measuring sets: tape measures, rulers and rolling guides are other essential pieces of kit for the cake decorator. In order to accurately measure fondants, cakes, widths and depths you should always have to hand a set of accurate measuring tools.

Ribbons of all sizes are great for tying around cakes for an elegant finish.

Piping Work

Piping icing can be a daunting task for anyone new to cake decorating. It's a skill that takes a lot of practice to get right.

Once mastered, it will allow the cake decorator to perform a wide range of creative tasks, including scalloping and creating swags, ropes, flowers, leaves and many other effects.

Make the royal icing as per the recipe on page 27, and ensure that it's kept in an airtight container to prevent it from hardening and drying out. The royal icing needs to be stiff enough to hold its form, yet malleable enough to be piped through a small piping nozzle.

How to make a piping bag and pipe royal icing:

1. Take a large square of greaseproof paper and fold diagonally in half.

2. Use a palette knife/scissors to cut down the fold.

3. With the longest side of the triangle facing you, fold one of the corners up and around to meet the top point of the triangle.

4. Holding it in place, bring the other corner around to face the cone shape.

5. Secure the top by folding the rim of the open end in on itself – you can staple it into place if that's easier.

6. Cut the point off the cone to accommodate the size of the piping nozzle you are using. Insert the piping nozzle and secure in place with a piping bag collar.

7. Fill the bag with royal icing.

8. Press the open end together and fold over to stop the icing from spilling out.

9. Take a sheet of greaseproof paper and practise your piping patterns before you attempt to pipe directly onto a cake.

10. Practise swirls, swags and dotting and experiment with different piping nozzles to get practised in creating the effects you can achieve using this method of cake decorating.

11. Once you feel confident enough, pipe the patterns you want to create onto your cake.

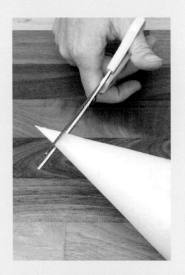

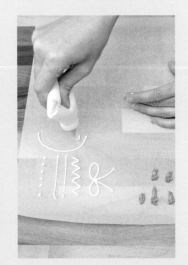

Fondant Icing Work

Fondant icing is the basis for many different cake decorating techniques and is a durable, malleable and extremely versatile material. It can be used to ice cakes and make novelty figures, flowers, plaques and decorations.

Fondant can be purchased at most supermarkets and all good cake decorating shops. Like with marzipan, it's worth buying good-quality fondant as it will keep for longer.

Fondant icing can be easily dyed using food dye, and will harden when left open in the air to make a smooth surface ideal for decorating and painting.

How to use fondant icing:

1. Knead the block of fondant on a silicone mat until it's soft and malleable – this will make it easier to roll and use for modelling.

2. Use gel food dye, adding a little at a time and knead it into the fondant. Continue kneading until the dye is evenly spread.

3. To cover a cake, measure the sides and diameter / width and ensure that you have enough fondant rolled out to cover the top and sides of the cake.

4. When rolled out, use a rolling pin to drape the fondant sheet over the cake.

5. Smooth the icing over the cake using your hands.

6. Use cake buffers dusted with a little icing sugar to achieve a smooth, professional finish.

7. Trim any excess with a sharp knife.

8. Rolled fondant can be used to make cut out shapes and plaques and can also be used to cover cake boards.

Basic Recipes

Vanilla Sponge

Serves 6 **Prep time** 15–20 minutes **Cooking time** 40–45 minutes

Ingredients

450 g / 1 lb / 3 cups self-raising
flour, sifted

450 g / 1 lb / 3 cups unsalted
butter, softened

450 g / 1 lb / 3 cups caster
(superfine) sugar

8 medium eggs, lightly beaten

2 tsp vanilla extract or seeds of
1 vanilla pod

a pinch of salt

Method

1. Preheat the oven to 170°C (150°C fan) / 325F / gas 3.
2. Grease and line two 20 cm (8 in) square tins with greaseproof paper.
3. Whisk the butter, sugar and vanilla in a bowl until pale and fluffy.
4. Add the eggs, a little at a time, and whisk on low speed.
5. Gently fold the flour into the egg and butter mixture.
6. Divide the batter evenly between the prepared cake tins.
7. Bake for 35–40 minutes until golden and risen and a skewer comes out clean from their centres.
8. Remove from the oven and let the sponges cool in their tins for 10 minutes before turning out onto a wire rack to cool completely; peel off any stuck greaseproof paper at this point.
9. Wrap well and set aside for filling and decorating.

Chocolate Sponge

Serves 8 **Prep time** 10–15 minutes **Cooking time** 40–45 minutes

Ingredients

225 g / 8 oz / 1 cup butter, softened

225 g / 8 oz / 1 cup caster (superfine) sugar

4 medium eggs, lightly beaten

225 g / 8 oz / 1 ½ cups self-raising flour, sifted

4 tbsp cocoa powder (sifted in with flour)

Method

1. Preheat oven to 180°C (160°C fan) / 425F / gas 4.
2. Line a tin with greaseproof paper.
3. Whisk together the butter and sugar until pale and fluffy.
4. Add the eggs slowly and combine, ensuring that the mix does not curdle. If the mix curdles, add a small amount of the flour and continue.
5. Add the flour and cocoa mix and slowly combine or fold in.
6. Spoon the mixture into the tin.
7. Place in oven for 30–35 minutes or until a skewer comes out clean when inserted.
8. Turn out onto a wire rack to cool completely. Remove the greaseproof paper from the sponge.
9. Wrap the cake and set aside for later use.

Round Fruit Cake

Serves 25 **Prep time** 20–30 minutes **Cooking time** 2 hours 30 minutes

Ingredients

200 g / 7 oz / 1 cup currants

100 g / 3 ½ oz / ½ cup sultanas

100 g / 3 ½ oz / ½ cup raisins

65 g / 2 ½ oz / ⅓ cup glacé cherries, quartered

50 g / 1 ¾ oz / ¼ cup mixed peel

50 g / 1 ¾ oz / ⅓ cup blanched almonds

½ lemon, zest grated

175 g / 6 oz / 1 ⅙ cups plain (all-purpose) flour

½ tsp ground cinnamon

¼ tsp ground mixed spice

150 g / 5 oz / ¾ cup butter

150 g / 5 oz / ¾ cup soft brown sugar

2 large eggs

1 tsp black treacle

3 tbsp brandy

Method

1. Preheat the oven to 150°C (130°C fan) / 300F / gas 2.
2. Line a 15 cm (6 in) square cake tin with two layers of greaseproof paper.
3. Combine currants, sultanas, raisins, glacé cherries, mixed peel, almonds and lemon zest and mix.
4. Sift the flour and spices together into a bowl.
5. Cream the butter and sugar in another bowl until light and fluffy.
6. Add the eggs one at a time following each one with one spoon of flour.
7. Fold in the remaining ingredients, except the brandy, and mix well.
8. Spoon the mixture into the tin, spread level and make a slight hollow in the centre of the mixture to ensure the cake stays flat during baking.
9. Tie two layers of brown paper around the outside of the tin, then bake for 2 hours 30 minutes.
10. Remove from the oven and allow to cool in the tin.
11. Turn out the cake onto a wire rack and prick all over with a metal skewer.
12. Spoon over the brandy, wrap well and store until needed.

Cupcakes

Makes 24 **Prep time** 25 minutes **Cooking time** 15–20 minutes

Ingredients

For the cupcakes:

225 g / 8 oz / 1 cup butter softened

225 g / 8 oz / 1 cup caster (superfine) sugar

4 medium eggs, beaten

225 g / 8 oz / 1 ½ cups self-raising flour

½ vanilla pod, seeds only

For the buttercream:

250 g / 9 oz / 1 ⅙ cups butter

a pinch of salt

vanilla seeds

350 g / 12 oz / 3 cups icing
  (confectioners') sugar, sieved

food dye

Method

1. Preheat the oven to 190°C (170°C fan) / 375F / gas 5.
2. Line two 12-hole muffin tins with cupcake cases.
3. In a mixing bowl beat together the butter and sugar with an electric whisk until pale and fluffy.
4. Slowly add the eggs a little at a time while beating the mixture on medium speed.
5. Add the flour and vanilla and combine on a low speed, or fold in using a large spoon.
6. Pipe or spoon the mix into the cake cases until they are two-thirds full, making sure not to get any mix on the side of the cases.
7. Place the trays in the oven and bake for 12–15 minutes or until firm to the touch.
8. Cool the cakes slightly in the tin and place on a wire rack to cool completely.
9. To make the buttercream, beat the butter, salt and vanilla in a bowl.
10. Add the icing sugar a spoon at a time, beating to incorporate between each spoonful.
11. Once all the icing sugar has been added, incorporate the food dye and beat the mix on high speed for 3–4 minutes until light and fluffy.
12. Using a large star-shaped nozzle, pipe swirls, starting from the outside of the cake, into the centre.

Classic Victoria Sponge

Serves 8 **Prep time** 25 minutes **Cooking time** 20 minutes

Ingredients

225 g / 8 oz / 1 cup caster (superfine) sugar

225 g / 8 oz / 1 cup butter, softened

4 eggs, beaten

225 g / 8 oz / 1 ½ cups self-raising flour

1 tsp baking powder

2 tbsp milk

For the filling:

150 g / 5 oz / ¾ cup strawberry jam (jelly)

300 ml / 10 ½ fl. oz / 1 ¼ cups fresh whipping cream

icing (confectioners') sugar to dust

Method

1. Preheat the oven to 190°C (170°C fan) / 375F / gas 5.
2. Line two 20 cm (8 in) round cake tins with greaseproof paper.
3. Beat all the cake ingredients together in a bowl until smooth.
4. Divide the mix between the tins and smooth with the back of a spoon.
5. Bake in oven for 20 minutes or until golden and the cake springs back when pressed lightly.
6. Remove from oven and allow to cool in the tin for 10 minutes.
7. Turn the cakes onto a wire rack and allow to cool completely.
8. Spread one sponge with jam and the other with cream, then sandwich together. Dust with icing sugar and serve.

Basic Chocolate Log

Serves 8 **Prep time** 30 minutes **Cooking time** 30–35 minutes

Ingredients

For the sponge cake:

250 g / 9 oz / 1 ¼ cups unsalted
butter, softened

250 g / 9 oz / 1 ¼ cups castor (superfine) sugar

4 medium eggs, lightly beaten

250 g / 9 oz / 1 ¼ cups self-raising flour

4 tbsp cocoa powder

For the chocolate buttercream:

125 g / 4 ½ oz / ½ cup unsalted
butter, softened

175 g / 6 oz / 1 ½ cups icing (confectioners')
sugar, sifted

100 g / 3 ½ oz / ²/₃ cup dark chocolate, melted

Method

1. Preheat oven to 180°C (160°C fan) / 350F / gas 4.
2. Grease and line a swiss-roll tin with greaseproof paper.
3. Whisk together butter and sugar until pale and fluffy.
4. Add the eggs slowly and combine.
5. Sieve the flour and cocoa together, then fold into the butter mix.
6. Tip the mixture into the tin and spread level. Bake in oven for 30–35 minutes or until springy to the touch.
7. Allow the cake to slightly cool in the tin.
8. Whilst the cake is cooling, dampen a tea towel and place on a chopping board.
9. Carefully turn out the sponge onto the towel on the board.
10. Trim the sponge and then score along the short edge, about 1 cm (½ in) deep to help with starting the roll.
11. Cream together the butter and sugar in a large mixing bowl until pale and thick.
12. Whisk in the melted chocolate in a slow, steady stream until thoroughly incorporated.
13. Once the sponge has cooled completely, spread with buttercream filling.
14. Starting with the scored edge, carefully roll the sponge to form a log shape.

Chocolate Collar Cake

Makes 1 **Prep time** 10–15 minutes

Ingredients

Round sponge cake or chocolate sponge
    20 cm (8 in)

125 g / 4 ½ oz / ¾ cup milk or dark chocolate

30 g / 1 oz / ¹/₅ cup white chocolate

400 g / 14 oz / 1 ¾ cups chocolate buttercream

1 strip greaseproof paper, cut slightly wider than
    the height of the cake and long enough to
    circle the cake

Method

1. Melt the different chocolates gently over separate bain-maries, making sure that the water doesn't touch the bottom of the bowls.
2. Cover the cake with chocolate buttercream, ensuring an even application.
3. When melted, drizzle the white chocolate in a random pattern across the strip of greaseproof paper and allow to cool and harden.
4. Spread the milk or dark chocolate over the strip of greaseproof paper with a palette knife.
5. Place the collar, milk or dark chocolate side down, around the cake, carefully adhering it to the buttercream, seal with a little tape and place in the refrigerator to set.
6. When the chocolate has hardened, carefully remove the greaseproof paper.
7. Trim the collar down with a heated sharp knife so that it provides a small lip.
8. Decorate with chocolate flakes.

Basic Macaroons

Makes 15 **Prep time** 40 minutes **Cooking time** 10–15 minutes

Ingredients

175 g / 6 oz / 1 ½ cups icing (confectioners')
sugar

125 g / 4 ½ oz / 1 cup ground almonds

3 large egg whites, at room temperature

75 g / 3 oz / ⅓ cup caster (superfine) sugar

food dye of choice

your filling of choice

Method

1. Preheat the oven to 140°C (120°C fan) / 275F / gas 1. On a sheet of greaseproof paper, use a pencil to draw 30 even-sized circles that are 2.5 cm (1 in) across. Turn the paper over and place on a baking tray.
2. Place the icing sugar and ground almonds in a food processor and pulse, then pass through a sieve, discarding anything left in the sieve.
3. In a clean bowl, whisk the egg whites until they form soft peaks. Add the caster sugar and whisk until thick and glossy and stiff peaks are formed.
4. Add any dyes or extracts. Fold in half the almond mix, using a spatula.
5. Add the remaining almonds and continue folding until everything is fully mixed together.
6. Transfer the mixture to a piping bag with a 1 cm (½ in) diameter round nozzle and pipe onto the baking trays, using the circles as a guide.
7. Tap the baking trays firmly on a work surface to expel any air bubbles. Leave to stand to 10–15 minutes.
8. Bake in the oven for 10–15 minutes. Remove and allow to cool completely before removing from the baking tray and filling.

Chocolate Ganache

Makes enough to cover 20 cm (8 in) cake **Prep time** 10–15 minutes

Ingredients

225 g / 8 oz / 1 ½ cups dark chocolate
    (maximum 55% cocoa solids)
175 ml / 6 fl. oz / ¾ cup double (heavy) cream

Method

1. In a heatproof bowl, break the chocolate into small pieces.
2. In a pan, bring the cream to a rolling boil and then remove from the heat.
3. Pour the cream straight onto the chocolate pieces.
4. Stir the mix vigorously to combine.
5. Set the mixture aside to cool or use straightaway if covering a cake.
6. If the ganache has been chilled, bring it up to room temperature and whisk before using.

Royal Icing

Makes enough to cover 20 cm (8 in) round cake **Prep time** 10–15 minutes

Ingredients

675 g / 1 lb 8 oz / 6 cups icing (confectioners')
    sugar

3 egg whites

2–3 teaspoons of strained lemon juice

Method

1. Sift the icing sugar.
2. In a clean bowl, whisk the egg whites until just frothy.
3. Add half the icing sugar and beat with the egg whites, using a wooden spoon.
4. Add the lemon juice and half the remaining icing sugar, then continue beating until the icing is smooth and white.
5. Add the rest of the icing sugar a little at a time until soft peaks are formed.
6. The icing can now be divided and dyed as required.
7. Store the icing in an airtight container until needed.

Cake Decorating

Chocolate Cakes

Chocolate Ice Cream Terrine

Serves 6–8 **Prep time** 2 hours

Ingredients

200 g / 7 oz / 1 ⅓ cups dark chocolate, melted

110 g / 4 oz / ⅔ cup white chocolate, melted

500 ml / 17 fl. oz / 1 pint dark chocolate ice cream

300 ml / 10 ½ fl. oz / 1 ¼ cups milk chocolate ice cream

edible gold leaf

Method

1. Spread three quarters of the dark chocolate over a piece of cling film and use it to line a terrine mould.
2. Use the rest of the chocolate to coat thin strips of cling film, then wrap them around a glass to form the ribbons. Leave the chocolate to set.
3. Spread the white chocolate over a piece of cling film and leave to set. Cut it into rounds with a pastry cutter.
4. Fill the terrine with half of the dark chocolate ice cream and hollow out a channel in the centre.
5. Fill with the milk chocolate ice cream, then top with the rest of the dark chocolate ice cream.
6. Freeze until firm and then turn out onto a serving plate. Decorate the terrine with the chocolate ribbons, white chocolate circles and gold leaf.

Chocolate Rose Cake

Serves 8 **Prep time** 1 hour

Ingredients

chocolate sponge cake (see page 19)

400 g / 14 oz / 2 cups dark chocolate
    fondant icing

110 g / 4 oz / $^2/_3$ cup dark chocolate, melted

Method

1. Knead the chocolate fondant icing until pliable.
2. Divide the fondant icing into about 8 even-sized pieces. Roll out a piece of fondant on a sheet of greaseproof paper to make a long, wide strip. Spread the centre of the cake with melted chocolate.
3. Start rolling the edge of the fondant strip into a tight curl.
4. Transfer it to the top of the cake and continue to wrap the fondant ribbon loosely around.
5. Build up the layers with more strips until the whole of the top of the cake is covered.

Cherry Chocolate Fan Cake

Serves 8 **Prep time** 1 hour

Ingredients

chocolate sponge cake (see page 19)

2 quantities chocolate ganache
(see page 26)

110 g / 4 oz / ½ cup apricot jam (jelly)

200 g / 7 oz / 1 cup dark chocolate
fondant icing

6 fresh cherries, stoned

icing (confectioners') sugar to dust

edible gold leaf

Method

1. Melt the jam in the microwave, then brush over the top and sides of the cake. Pour the chocolate ganache on top of the cake and use a palette knife to smooth it down the sides.
2. Knead the chocolate fondant icing until pliable and roll out on a non-stick mat. Cut the icing into strips and cut the edges at an angle.
3. Ripple the icing with your fingers, then spread one side out to create a fan.
4. Pinch the bottom of the fan to secure. Arrange half of the fans around the edge of the cake. Arrange the rest of the fans in a ring on top of the cake.
5. Dust the fan ring lightly with icing sugar. Spoon the cherries into the centre and finish with some gold leaf.

Chocolate Curl Cake

Serves 8 **Prep time** 1 hour

Ingredients

round chocolate sponge cake (see page 19)

110 g / 4 oz / ½ cup apricot jam (jelly)

400 g / 14 oz / 2 cups dark chocolate,
    melted

Method

1. Melt the jam in the microwave, then brush over the top and sides of the cake.
2. Pour three quarters of the melted chocolate on top of the cake.
3. Use a palette knife to smooth the top and spread it evenly down the sides and leave to chill.
4. Spread the rest of the chocolate in a thin layer onto a marble slab. Leave to set.
5. Create curls by pushing a flat-bladed knife over the surface of the chocolate.
6. Place the curls onto the cake.

Chocolate Biscuit Cake

Serves 6 **Prep time** 1 hour

Ingredients

225 g / 8 oz / 1 cup dark chocolate, melted

6 round biscuits

400 g / 14 oz / 2 cups chocolate ganache (see page 26)

150 g / 5 oz / 1 cup raspberries

Method

1. Using a third of the chocolate, spread spoonfuls on a sheet of cling film to make six 8 cm (3 in) round medallions. Leave to set.
2. Place the biscuits onto six serving plates. Coat the biscuit bases with the rest of the chocolate.
3. Pipe the ganache in a spiral around the chocolate biscuit.
4. Reserve 6 raspberries for decoration and pile the rest in the centre of the biscuits. Pipe the rest of the ganache to encase the raspberries in a big swirl.
5. Peel the chocolate medallions off of the cling film and set on top of the ganache.
6. Top with the reserved raspberries for decoration.

Chocolate Bay Leaf Cake

Serves 8 **Prep time** 1 hour 30 minutes

Ingredients

round chocolate sponge cake (see page 19)

110 g / 4 oz / 1 cup dark chocolate, chopped

7 fresh bay leaves

8 hazelnuts (cobnuts)

200 g / 7 oz / 1 cup granulated sugar

2 tbsp icing (confectioners') sugar

Method

1. Melt the chocolate in a microwave or bain-marie. Paint the melted chocolate onto the back of the bay leaves and leave to set.
2. Carefully peel away the leaves from the chocolate.
3. Stick a cocktail stick into each hazelnut to help coat them in the caramel.
4. Put the granulated sugar in a heavy-bottomed saucepan and heat until it starts to melt around the edges. Gently swirl the pan over the heat until the sugar has all melted and lightly browned.
5. Dip the hazelnuts into the caramel and leave them to drip upside down over the pan until the caramel has hardened.
6. Dust the cake with icing sugar. Assemble the leaves and caramel-coated hazelnuts on top of the cake.

White Chocolate and Cherry Cake

Serves 8 **Prep time** 1 hour 30 minutes

Ingredients

chocolate sponge cake (see page 19)

400 g can of cherries in syrup

175 ml / 6 fl. oz / ¾ cup double (heavy) cream

300 g / 10 ½ oz / 2 cups white chocolate, broken into pieces

30 g / 1 oz / ¼ cup good-quality dark chocolate

a few fresh cherries for decoration

2 fresh rose leaves

Method

1. Heat the syrup from the tin of cherries in a pan and boil until it reduces by half.
2. Bring the double cream to a rolling boil and then pour onto 225 g / 8 oz / 1 ½ cups of the white chocolate. Stir the chocolate until it has all melted and formed a glossy ganache (see page 26).
3. Melt the dark chocolate slowly in a bowl over a pan of simmering water. Wash and thoroughly dry the fresh cherries and then partially dip them in the chocolate. Set them on greaseproof paper to set.
4. Using a small brush, paint the chocolate onto the smooth surface of the rose leaf and place on the paper to set.
5. Slice the cake in half horizontally and brush with the reduced syrup. Scatter the tinned cherries onto the sponge.
6. Smooth over a layer of ganache and place the remaining cake slice on top.
7. Melt the remaining white chocolate and pour some onto a marble slab, retaining some to cover the cake. Using a palette knife, smooth the chocolate over the marble until it sets. Create curls by pushing a flat-bladed knife over the surface of the white chocolate.
8. Cover the cake in the remaining ganache and then pour the remaining melted white chocolate onto the top of the cake.
9. Stick the curls onto the side of the cake. Add the chocolate-dipped cherries on top.
10. Carefully remove the leaves from the chocolate and place them on to the cake. Tie a ribbon around the outside of the cake.

Chocolate, Pear and Chestnut Gateau

Serves 8 **Prep time** 1 hour 30 minutes

Ingredients

round chocolate sponge cake
  (see page 19)

3 pears, peeled

1 cinnamon stick

55 g / 2 oz / ¼ cup butter

55 g / 2 oz / ¼ cup demerara sugar

400 g / 14 oz / 1 ¾ cups sweetened
  chestnut purée

110 g / 4 oz dark chocolate, melted

marrons glacés

icing (confectioners') sugar to dust

Method

1. Cover the pears and cinnamon with water and poach for 10 minutes or until soft. Drain the pears, then cut 2 of them in half and remove the cores.
2. Return the pear halves to the pan with the butter and sugar and cook over a low heat until the sugar has dissolved and the pears are lightly caramelised.
3. Leave the pears to cool and then slice them thinly.
4. Divide the cake and fill with a third of the chestnut purée, then cover the top and sides with the remainder.
5. Fan the pear slices around the outside of the cake and then pour on the melted chocolate. Spread out using a palette knife.
6. Arrange the marrons glacés and the reserved poached pear on top of the cake. Dust the cake with icing sugar.

Chocolate Truffle Cake

Serves 8 **Prep time** 2 hours

Ingredients

square chocolate sponge cake
  (see page 19)

110 g / 4 oz / 1 cup dark chocolate, melted

400 g / 14 oz / 1 ¾ cups chocolate ganache
  (see page 26)

2 tbsp unsweetened cocoa powder

edible gold leaf

Method

1. Spread the melted dark chocolate onto a sheet of greaseproof paper and leave to set. Use a small ice cream scoop to form a ball of ganache and reserve.
2. Spread the rest of the ganache over the top and sides of the cake. Dust the cake with cocoa powder.
3. Carefully lift the chocolate sheet off of the greaseproof paper and break into shards.
4. Stick the chocolate shards into the centre of the cake.
5. Dust the reserved ganache truffle with cocoa powder and set it in the centre of the chocolate shards.
6. Use a dry brush to apply the edible gold leaf to the truffle.

Chocolate Orange Ribbon Cake

Serves 8 **Prep time** 3 hours **Cooking time** 35 minutes

Ingredients

110 g / 4 oz / 1 cup self-raising flour, sifted

110 g / 4 oz / ½ cup caster (superfine) sugar

110 g / 4 oz / ½ cup butter, softened

2 large eggs

2 tbsp orange zest, finely grated

150 g / 5 oz / 1 cup chocolate chips

1 chocolate girolle and cutter

225 g / 8 oz / 1 cup buttercream

Method

1. Preheat the oven to 190°C (170°C fan) / 375F / gas 5 and line a 20 cm (8 in) round tin with greaseproof paper. Prepare and measure all of the ingredients.
2. Combine the flour, sugar, butter, eggs and half of the orange zest in a bowl and whisk together for 2 minutes or until smooth, then fold in the chocolate chips.
3. Spoon the mixture into the tin and bake for 35 minutes. Once cooked, transfer the cake to a wire rack and leave to cool completely.
4. Use a chocolate roll cutting wheel to shave the chocolate girolle into delicate ribbons.
5. Spread the top of the cake with buttercream. Sprinkle over the remaining orange zest.
6. From the centre, stick the chocolate ribbons into the buttercream. Build the layers until the top of the cake is covered and then spread out the ribbons.

Chocolate and Raspberry Gateau

Serves 8 **Prep time** 1 hour 30 minutes

Ingredients

round chocolate sponge cake
  (see page 19)

400 g / 14 oz / 1 ¾ cups chocolate ganache
  (see page 26)

200 g / 7 oz / 1 cup whipped cream

2 tbsp raspberry jam (jelly)

200 g / 7 oz / 1 ¼ cups fresh raspberries

fresh mint leaves

icing (confectioners') sugar to dust

Method

1. Prepare and measure out all of the ingredients.
2. Fold 150 g / 5 oz / ⅔ cup of the chocolate ganache into the whipped cream. Cut the cake in half horizontally and sandwich together with the chocolate cream.
3. Spread the rest of the ganache over the top and sides of the cake. Use a palette knife to give a smooth, even finish.
4. Spread the raspberry jam over the top of the cake.
5. Position the raspberries on top of the cake.
6. Tuck the mint leaves in and around the raspberries. Dust the cake with icing sugar to finish.

Cherry and Chocolate Cheesecake

Serves 10 **Prep time** 1 hour

Ingredients

round chocolate sponge cake
(see page 19)

200 g / 7 oz / 1 cup granulated sugar

60 ml / 2 fl. oz / ¼ cup cherry syrup

150 g / 5 oz / 1 cup black cherries in syrup,
drained

600 g / 1 lb 5 oz / 2 ½ cups cream cheese

150 ml / 5 fl. oz / ½ cup double
(heavy) cream

110 g / 4 oz / ½ cup caster (superfine) sugar

1 lemon, zest and juice

Method

1. Put the granulated sugar in a heavy-bottomed saucepan and heat until it starts to melt around the edges. Gently swirl the pan over the heat until the sugar has all melted. Pour the caramel onto a non-stick baking mat. Leave to cool and harden.
2. Put the cake into a loose-bottomed plastic cake mould that fits exactly and brush with the cherry syrup. Space three quarters of the cherries out on top of the cake.
3. Beat the cream cheese with the cream, sugar and lemon zest and juice and spoon over the cherries. Spread the mixture out with a palette knife and chill for 2 hours.
4. Take the cake out of the mould and transfer to a serving plate. Top with the reserved cherries.
5. Smash the cooled caramel with a rolling pin. Stick the shards into the top of the cheesecake.

Violin Cake

Serves 4–6 **Prep time** 1 hour

Ingredients

1 litre / 1 ¾ pints / 4 cups chocolate
   ice cream

2 brandy snaps

50 g / 1 ¾ oz / ¼ cup chocolate fondant

20 g / ¾ oz / ⅛ cup green fondant
   (see pages 14–15)

20 g / ¾ oz / ⅛ cup red fondant
   (see pages 14–15)

20 g / ¾ oz / ⅛ cup royal icing
   (see page 27)

Method

1. On greaseproof paper draw a violin shape using an edible icing pen.
   Cut a block of ice cream into the shape of a violin and place in the freezer.
2. Heat the brandy snaps in the oven to uncurl. Remove from the
   oven and while they are still warm cut out a violin shape using the
   parchment template.
3. Roll and cut out a piece of chocolate fondant into the shape of the chin
   rest and neck of the violin.
4. Remove the ice cream violin from the freezer and arrange the chocolate
   fondant shapes and brandy snap shape on top.
5. Stamp out a leaf from the green fondant icing and create a rose from the
   red fondant icing. Fill a piping bag with the royal icing.
6. Pipe swirls onto the top of the neck to form the scroll and lines to represent
   the strings.

Chocolate Ganache and Raspberry Cake

Serves 10 **Prep time** 1 hour

Ingredients

3 chocolate sponge cakes
(see page 19)

400 g / 14 oz / 2 ⅔ cups dark chocolate,
melted

350 ml / 12 fl. oz / 1 ½ cups double (heavy)
cream, whipped

150 g / 5 oz / 1 cup raspberries

110 g / 4 oz / ⅔ cup white chocolate
shards

icing (confectioners') sugar to dust

Method

1. Spoon 50 g / 2 oz / ⅓ cup of the melted chocolate into a small piping bag and pipe squiggles onto a sheet of greaseproof paper. Leave to set.
2. Fold the rest of the melted chocolate into the whipped cream and spoon the mixture into a piping bag. Pipe large beads of the ganache onto the first cake to fill the entire surface (see pages 12–13).
3. Top with the second cake and repeat the beading to use up another third of the ganache.
4. Top with the third cake and pipe the rest of the ganache on top. Stud the cake with raspberries.
5. Position the white chocolate shards between the raspberries. Use a palette knife to lift the chocolate squiggles off the paper and transfer them carefully to the cake.
6. Dust the cake with a little icing sugar to finish.

Chocolate Rosebud Cake

Serves 8 **Prep time** 1 hour

Ingredients

round chocolate sponge cake
(see page 19)

110 g / 2 oz / ½ cup dark chocolate, melted

1 kg / 2 lbs 3 oz / 4 ½ cups dark chocolate
fondant icing

16 fresh roses

1 egg white, beaten

55 g / 2 oz / ¼ cup caster (superfine) sugar

1 tsp pink dusting powder

Method

1. Spread the cake with melted chocolate.
2. Cover with fondant icing, using a cake smoother to get a glossy, professional finish. Trim away any excess icing.
3. Remove the stalks from the roses.
4. Brush the roses with egg white.
5. Mix the caster sugar with the pink dusting powder and sprinkle onto the roses until they are completely covered, shaking off any excess.
6. Attach the roses to the cake with a little more melted chocolate.

Star Cupcakes Chocolate Cake

Serves 8–10 **Prep time** 1 hour 30 minutes

Ingredients

20 cm (8 in) round chocolate sponge
(see page 19)

8 cm (3 in) round chocolate sponge
(see page 19)

5 vanilla cupcakes (see page 21)

150 g / 5 oz / ¾ cup blue fondant icing
(see pages 14–15)

400 g / 14 oz / 1 ¾ cups vanilla buttercream

1 ¼ kg / 2 ¾ lbs / 6 cups white fondant icing
(see pages 14–15)

50 g / 2 oz / ¼ cup chocolate fondant icing

Method

1. Cover a 25 cm (10 in) cake board with blue fondant and allow to harden.
2. Cover the two sponges in buttercream and chill. Roll out 1 kg / 2 ¼ lb / 4 ¼ cups of the white fondant and cover both sponges. Smooth the white fondant and set the cakes aside to harden.
3. To make the decorations, roll out the chocolate and blue fondants and use star-shaped cutters to cut out stars in various sizes.
4. Place the remaining buttercream in a piping bag with a large star nozzle and pipe swirls onto the cupcakes. Decorate the cupcakes with some of the fondant stars.
5. Using edible glue, stick the fondant stars onto the sponges in a random pattern.
6. Place the larger cake onto the cake board and stack the smaller sponge on top. Fix a ribbon around the base of the bottom cake and arrange the cupcakes on top and on the bottom tier.

Chocolate Mask Cake

Serves 8 **Prep time** 1 hour

Ingredients

15 cm (6 in) round chocolate sponge
(see page 19)

250 g / 9 oz / 1 ½ cups dark chocolate,
for the mask

For the sauce:

250 g / 9 oz / 1 ½ cups good-quality dark
chocolate

70 ml / 2.4 fl. oz / ⅓ cup water

90 g / 3 oz / ½ cup granulated sugar

Method

1. Polish the inside of a Venetian party mask using dry cotton wool. Melt the chocolate for the mask over a bain-marie.
2. Pour the chocolate into the mask mould and coat the surface.
3. Once the mask has set, pour or brush another thin coat of chocolate to strengthen the mask. Once set, carefully peel away the mould. Boil the water and sugar in a saucepan until melted, then allow to cool.
4. Melt the chocolate for the sauce in a bain-marie. Remove from the heat. Add the syrup, a spoonful at a time, to the chocolate and whisk to combine, then allow to cool.
5. Pour the cooled sauce over the cake.
6. Carefully position the mask onto the cake and light sparklers at the time of serving.

Cake Decorating

Indulgent Cakes

Coconut Cake

Serves 12 **Prep time** 30 minutes

Ingredients

For the sponge cake:

400 g / 1 lb / 2 cups caster (superfine) sugar

400 g / 1 lb / 4 cups self-raising flour

400 g / 1 lb / 2 cups butter, softened

8 medium eggs

80 g / 3 oz / 1 cup desiccated coconut

½ lemon, zested

For the coconut buttercream:

175 g / 6 oz / 1 ¼ cups icing
  (confectioners') sugar, sieved

250 g / 9 oz / 1 cup butter, softened

1 tbsp coconut syrup

40 g / 1 ½ oz / ½ cup desiccated coconut

Method

1. Line a 20 cm (8 in) cake tin and follow the method for making a basic sponge (see page 18), adding the coconut and lemon zest to the mixture.
2. Beat the icing sugar, butter and coconut syrup together to make a smooth buttercream.
3. When cooled, slice the cake in half and place the top half to one side.
4. Spread the bottom cake layer with a thick layer of the coconut buttercream.
5. Place the other half of the cake carefully on top. Coat the cake with buttercream and then sprinkle with dessicated coconut.

Fraisier

Serves 6 **Prep time** 1 hour 30 minutes

Ingredients

round vanilla sponge cake
(see page 18)

400 ml / 13 fl. oz / 1 ½ cups double
(heavy) cream

100 g / 3 ½ oz / 1 cup icing
(confectioners') sugar

400 g / 1 lb / 2 cups strawberries,
hulled and halved

2 leaves of gelatine

Method

1. Take a sponge and trim around the edge of the cake to remove the crust. Slice the cake horizontally to make 2 thin discs of sponge cake. Place one slice into a round baking tin that fits the cake exactly.
2. Whip the cream and icing sugar together until the mixture becomes stiff. Line the bottom slice of cake with strawberry halves and arrange a ring of strawberry halves around the inside of the tin.
3. Fill the tin with the whipped cream and smooth the top. Place in the refrigerator to allow the cream to firm.
4. Whilst chilling, soak the gelatine in some cold water. Blend the remaining strawberries and pass them through a sieve to extract the juice and remove the seeds. Gently heat in a pan.
5. Remove the gelatine from the water and add to the strawberry juice and stir until dissolved. Remove from the heat and pour into a bowl sitting on some ice. When cool, remove from the chilling bowl and mix in 1 tbsp of double cream.
6. Take the tin from the refrigerator and place the last sponge slice on top. When the strawberry jelly is almost set, pour over the last sponge tier. Chill to set and then remove the cake from the tin and decorate with any leftover cream and strawberries.

Apple Bavarian

Serves 4–6 **Prep time** 1 hour 15 minutes (plus setting time)

Ingredients

For the Bavarian:

3 apples, peeled, cored and quartered

½ lemon, juiced

30 g / 1 oz / ⅛ cup butter

100 g / 3 ½ oz / ½ cup granulated sugar

4 egg yolks, beaten

200 ml / 6 ½ fl oz / ¾ cup milk

60 g / 2 oz / ¼ cup honey

100 g / 3 ½ oz / ¾ cup maple syrup

4 sheets of gelatine

300 ml / 10 fl. oz / 1 ¼ cups double (heavy) cream

For the decoration:

250 g / 9 oz / 1 ¼ cup granulated sugar

3 tbsp water

walnut halves

Method

1. Cover the apple segments in lemon juice to stop them going brown. Melt the butter and sugar in a wide frying pan. Sauté the apples until golden brown. Remove from the heat and allow to cool.
2. Mix the beaten egg yolks with the milk, honey and maple syrup and heat gently in a saucepan. Meanwhile, soften the gelatine in cold water and wring it out.
3. Add the gelatine to the egg, milk, honey and syrup mixture. Stir continuously until it dissolves. Pour into a bowl and stir in the cream and combine. Allow to cool by sitting the bowl inside a larger bowl of iced water.
4. Line a 15–20 cm (6–8 in) loose-based tin with cling film. Place the apple segments around the sides and base of the tin. Pour in the cream mixture and place in the refrigerator for 3 hours to set.
5. In a pan, mix the sugar and water together and heat over a high heat until the mixture begins to caramelise. Using a fork, very carefully dip the walnut halves into the syrup and place on a greaseproof sheet to cool.
6. Using a fork, drizzle the remaining syrup across a sheet of greaseproof paper into a pattern. Allow to set for 3 hours. Decorate the Bavarian with the walnuts and sugar crackling.

Pistachio and Cherry Cake

Serves 4–6 **Prep time** 1 hour 15 minutes

Ingredients

For the sponge:

150 g / 5 oz / 1 ¼ cups shelled, unsalted pistachios

3 egg whites

150 g / 5 oz / ²/₃ cup caster (superfine) sugar

100 g / 3 ½ oz / 1 cup plain (all-purpose) flour

1 tsp baking powder

a pinch of salt

100 g / 3 ½ oz / ½ cup butter

green food dye

2–3 tbsp large-grain sugar

4 green glacé cherries

angelica to decorate

For tho buttorcroam:

100 g / 3 ½ oz / ½ cup butter, melted

160 g / 5 oz / 1 ½ cups icing (confectioners') sugar, sifted

green food dye

60 g / 2 oz shelled, unsalted pistachios

Method

1. Place the pistachios in a food processor and pulse until they form a fine powder.
2. In a mixing bowl, beat the egg whites and sugar for 5 minutes until thick and creamy.
3. Sift the flour, baking powder and salt into another bowl. Add one third of the flour mix to the egg mixture and fold, then gently fold in 80 g / 3 oz / ¾ cup of the powdered pistachios.
4. Add the melted butter before folding in the rest of the flour and two drops of green food dye.
5. Spoon the mixture into a 18 cm (7 in) square cake tin and bake for 30–35 minutes at 180ºC (160ºC fan) / 350F / gas 4.
6. For the buttercream, beat the butter and the icing sugar in a mixing bowl until it is light and fluffy.
7. Add the green food dye a little at a time to reach the desired shade. Fold in the remaining powdered pistachios.
8. Slice the cake into three layers and sandwich the layers with buttercream.
9. Dust the top of the cake with large grains of sugar.
10. Decorate the cake with green glacé cherries and strips of angelica.

Kiwi and Almond Cake

Serves 8 **Prep time** 1 hour 30 minutes

Ingredients

vanilla and fruit sponge cake, loaf-shaped
(see page 18)

500 g / 17 oz / 1 ¾ cups buttercream

1 tsp almond essence

40 g / 1 ½ oz / ¼ cup ground almonds

4 kiwi fruit, peeled and sliced

silver leaves for decoration

15 raspberries

sugar balls

Method

1. When baking the vanilla sponge, add your chosen fruits to the mixture before baking.
2. Whip the buttercream with the almond essence and ground almonds.
3. Slice the sponge loaf horizontally and spread with the almond buttercream using a palette knife.
4. Carefully sandwich the sponge layers together. Coat the cake with more of the almond cream.
5. Place the kiwi slices onto the sides and top of the cake.
6. Position the silver leaves on the top of the cake.
7. Decorate with the raspberries and sugar balls.

Gooseberry, Peach and White Chocolate Cake

Serves 4 **Prep time** 1 hour 30 minutes

Ingredients

round Victoria sponge filled with apricot jam (see page 22)

125 g / 4 ½ / 1 cup white chocolate

chocolate transfer sheet

400 g / 14 oz / 2 cups buttercream

1 punnet of cape gooseberries (physalis)

1 small orange

2 firm peaches

Method

1. Melt the white chocolate gently over a bain-marie. When melted, spread most of the chocolate over the back of the chocolate transfer sheet.
2. Coat the cake with buttercream, ensuring even coverage. Wrap the transfer around the cake carefully. Place in the refrigerator to chill and set.
3. Meanwhile, dip the cape gooseberries into the remaining white chocolate and allow to set on greaseproof paper.
4. When the chocolate has hardened, carefully remove the acetate backing from the chocolate transfer sheet to leave the pattern showing.
5. Using a zesting tool, make some fine orange peel. Arrange the cape gooseberries across the top of the cake.
6. Slice the peaches into thin wedges and arrange among the cape gooseberries. Scatter with fine orange peel and serve.

Raspberry Mousse Cake

Serves 8 **Prep time** 1 hour

Ingredients

vanilla sponge cake, heart-shaped and split into 3 horizontally (see page 18)

55 g / 2 oz / ¼ cup light pink fondant icing (see pages 14–15)

55 g / 2 oz / ¼ cup dark pink fondant icing (see pages 14–15)

2 tsp powdered gelatine

400 g / 14 oz / 2 ½ cups raspberries

4 tbsp caster (superfine) sugar

200 ml / 6 ½ fl. oz / ¾ cup double (heavy) cream, whipped

Method

1. Roll out the light and dark pink fondant icing and cut out a heart shape from each.
2. Dissolve the gelatine in some warm water. Blend three quarters of the raspberries to a purée and strain into a saucepan. Heat the raspberry purée with the caster sugar until it dissolves.
3. Pour the raspberry purée and sugar mixture into a bowl and stir in half of the gelatine until it dissolves.
4. Put one of the cakes back into its tin and pour half of the raspberry purée mixture on top. Chill until set. Fold the other half of the raspberry mixture into the whipped cream with the rest of the gelatine to form the mousse.
5. Spoon a third of the mousse onto the base cake. Top with the middle cake and spread with another third of the mousse.
6. Top with the jelly cake layer and arrange 2 fondant hearts on top. Spoon the remaining mousse into a piping bag and pipe around the edge of the cake. Top with raspberries. Chill and set for 2 hours.

Sugared Rose Cake

Serves 6 **Prep time** 15 minutes

Ingredients

round vanilla sponge cake (see page 18)

icing (confectioners') sugar for dusting

handful of fresh rose petals

1 egg white

30 g / 1 oz / ¼ cup caster (superfine) sugar

5 basil leaves

Method

1. Trim the edges and top of the sponge cake.
2. Dust the top with a liberal amount of icing sugar.
3. Gently brush the rose petals with egg white, then coat them in the caster sugar, ensuring a thorough coating. Allow to dry.
4. Gently brush the basil leaves with egg white.
5. Thoroughly coat the leaves in the caster sugar and allow to dry.
6. Arrange the petals and leaves on the cake and serve.

Mini Butterfly Cakes

Serves 4 **Prep time** 1 hour

Ingredients

four 8 cm (3 in) vanilla sponge cakes
   (see page 18)

icing (confectioners') sugar to dust

600 g / 1 lb 7 oz / 3 cups dyed fondant icing
   (see pages 14–15)

300 g / 10 oz / 1 ½ cups buttercream

ribbon

silk butterflies

Method

1. Dust a surface with icing sugar and roll out the fondant to cover four
    10 cm (4 in) cake boards. Brush the cake boards with water to moisten,
    then use a rolling pin to lay fondant on the boards.
2. Using a paddle tool or smoother, smooth over the surface of the fondant
    to help it stick and to remove any imperfections. Use a sharp knife to trim
    the sides and set aside.
3. Coat each cake with buttercream using a palette knife.
4. Cover each cake in different shades of fondant and use the smoother to
    remove any imperfections. Set aside and allow to harden.
5. Once the fondant is dry, carefully lift the cakes onto the cake boards and
    fix a length of ribbon around the cakes using double-sided adhesive tape.
6. Fix another length of ribbon around the boards. Place the silk butterflies
    on top of the cakes for decoration.

Mini Rose Cake

Serves 1 **Prep time** 1 hour

Ingredients

8 cm (3 in) square vanilla sponge cake (see page 18)

55 g / 2 oz / ¼ cup buttercream

55 g / 2 oz / ¼ cup red fondant icing (see pages 14–15)

110 g / 4 oz / ½ cup white fondant icing (see pages 14–15)

icing (confectioners') sugar to dust

55 g / 2 oz / ¼ cup green royal icing (see pages 14–15)

red ribbon

Method

1. Spread the top and the sides of the cake with buttercream.
2. Roll out the red fondant icing and cut out 4 small hearts.
3. Use the rest of the fondant to make the rose. Flatten small balls of the paste between cling film and use to make the petals.
4. Assemble the rose with a dab of water.
5. Knead the white fondant, then roll out on a work surface that has been lightly dusted with icing sugar.
6. Use the rolling pin to transfer the icing to the cake and mould it down and around the sides.
7. Use a cake smoother to get a smooth, professional finish to the icing.
8. Use a crimping tool to scallop the bottom edge of the icing.
9. Wrap the ribbon around the cake, attaching with a small blob of icing.
10. Pipe 3 leaves onto the top of the cake with the royal icing. Attach the roses and hearts with a small blob of icing.

Hand-painted Cake

Serves 6 **Prep time** 1 hour 30 minutes

Ingredients

vanilla sponge cake (see page 18)

500 g / 1 lb 3 oz / 2 cups white fondant
  icing

edible food dusts, various shades

rejuvenator spirit

ribbon, to decorate

Method

1. Draw a design on parchment using an icing pen.
2. Carefully lay the design on the cake and, using a scribing tool, prick the cake along the lines of the design.
3. Remove the parchment and, using the icing pen, draw a faint outline along the marks in the fondant.
4. Take the different shades of dust and mix with rejuvenator spirit.
5. Use a thin brush to paint the outline of the first part of the design.
6. Carefully fill in the lines using more dust and rejuvenator spirit.
7. Repeat step 5 and 6 for the rest of the design. Leave to dry for 2 hours.
8. Choose a complementary ribbon to fix along the bottom of the cake and secure using double-sided adhesive tape.

Coffee Macaroon Cake

Serves 6–8 **Prep time** 45 minutes

Ingredients

4 sheets gelatine

600 ml / 30 fl. oz / 3 cups double (heavy) cream

2 tsp coffee essence

200 g / 7 oz / 1 cup caster (superfine) sugar

12 small chocolate-filled macaroons (see page 25)

2 tsp gold sugar balls

1 pack of gold sugared almonds

small handful round, gold sweets

small handful chocolate-covered coffee beans

ribbon to decorate

Method

1. Soften the gelatine in cold water. Pour the cream, coffee essence and sugar into a saucepan and bring to the boil. Remove from the heat. Dissolve the gelatine into the cream mixture and stir.
2. Divide the mixture into two moulds, one wider than the other by at least the width of the macaroons.
3. Cool for 4 hours until the mixture in the moulds has set. Stand the moulds in a bowl of warm water, then carefully slide a palette knife around the edges.
4. Turn the larger mould out onto a serving plate and then turn out the second mould onto the middle of the top of the first.
5. Take one macaroon and push the gold balls around the rim.
6. Arrange the remaining macaroons around the circumference of the bottom layer.
7. Stand the sugared almonds against the sides of the top layer of the dessert.
8. Arrange the gold sweets and coffee beans around the top layer of the dessert.
9. Top off with the decorated macaroon. Tie a ribbon around the base layer and serve.

Sugar-spun Heart Cake

Serves 4 **Prep time** 45 minutes

Ingredients

vanilla sponge cake, heart-shaped
(see page 18)

100 g / 3 ½ oz / ½ cup caster (superfine)
sugar

40 ml / 1 ½ fl oz / ½ cup water

pink food dye

Method

1. Place the sugar and water in a heavy-bottomed saucepan and heat gently to form a syrup.
2. Slowly bring the syrup to a boil and when it begins to darken, remove the pan from the heat. Set the pan aside and allow to cool for 5 minutes.
3. Add a few drops of the pink food dye and stir.
4. Using a spoon, drizzle the syrup over 2 metal skewers in a backward and forward motion to form a nest.
5. When enough strands have formed and you have enough spun sugar to cover the cake, carefully remove the syrup from the skewers and place over the cake.

Iced Butterfly Cake

Serves 8 **Prep time** 2 hours

Ingredients

filled Victoria sponge cake (see page 22)

400 g / 13 oz / 2 cups purple fondant icing
(see pages 14–15)

icing pen

100 g / 4 oz / ½ cups royal icing
(see page 27)

edible copper shimmer dust

purple edible glitter gel

Method

1. Cover the filled Victoria sponge in rolled-out purple fondant and allow it to harden. Using an icing pen, draw a butterfly design on a piece of baking parchment.
2. Gently place the parchment onto the cake and use a scribing needle to mark a series of small holes along the pattern.
3. Remove the parchment and pipe royal icing along the dotted lines and allow to set.
4. Using a soft small brush, gently apply the shimmer dust inside the piped butterflies, then carefully pipe on the glitter gel.
5. Using a scriber needle, pull the gel out to the corners to match the butterfly design. To finish the cake, secure a ribbon around the base of the cake using adhesive tape.

Springtime Nut Cake

Serves 6 **Prep time** 1 hour

Ingredients

15 cm (6 in) vanilla sponge cake
  (see page 18)

250 g / 9 oz / 1 ¼ cups fondant icing
  (see pages 14–15)

green, pink, yellow and lilac food dye

250 g / 9 oz / 1 ¼ cups buttercream

100 g / 3 ½ oz / ¾ cup chopped roasted
  mixed nuts

50 g / 2 oz / ¼ cup royal icing
  (see page 27)

Method

1. Divide the fondant icing into quarters. Using the food dye, tint the fondant to make four different shades.
2. Roll out the fondants. Cut out and mould flowers and butterflies and allow to dry.
3. Coat the sponge in buttercream using a palette knife.
4. Gently pat the side of the cake with the chopped nuts to coat. Continue this around the entire side of the cake.
5. Using a cake comb, make a circular pattern in the top of the cake.
6. Arrange the flowers and butterflies on top of the cake. Pipe stems using green royal icing.

Shoe Cupcakes

Serves 12 **Prep time** 1 hour 15 minutes

Ingredients

12 cupcakes (see page 21)

350 g / 12 oz / 2 ¾ cups icing
(confectioners') sugar, sieved

250 g / 9 oz / 1 cup butter, softened

pink food dye

100 g / 4 oz / ½ cup white fondant icing
(see pages 14–15)

50g / 2 oz / ¼ cup royal icing (see page 27)

edible sparkles

glimmer sugar

sugar balls

Method

1. Beat the icing sugar and butter and a few drops of pink food dye together in a bowl until light and fluffy.
2. Transfer the buttercream into a piping bag with a large star nozzle. Pipe the buttercream onto the cupcakes. Start at the outside and work into the centre.
3. Roll out the white fondant, then carefully cut out 24 shoe soles using a template and 24 small lengths of fondant for the heels.
4. Place the soles on a staggered surface to form a raised shoe. Use royal icing to form the front of the shoe, then carefully pipe a thin line around the sides and back of the sole to build up the shoe.
5. Decorate the front of the shoe with edible sparkles and sugar balls. Shape the heels out of the remaining fondant and allow to set, then glue the heels to the underside of the soles using royal icing.
6. Decorate the cupcakes with the shoes, sparkles, glimmer sugar and sugar balls.

Cake Decorating

Celebration Cakes

Basket Weave Cake

Serves 4 **Prep time** 1 hour 30 minutes

Ingredients

fruit cake (see page 20)

500 g / 17 oz / 2 cups white fondant icing
   (see pages 14–15)

200 g / 7 oz / 1 cup buttercream

400 g / 14 oz / 1 ½ cups royal icing
   (see page 27)

selection of fresh seasonal flowers

Method

1. Use some of the fondant icing to cover a cake board slightly larger than the diameter of the cake.
2. Using a palette knife, coat the sponge in buttercream and place in the refrigerator to set.
3. Cover the cake in fondant icing and allow to dry. Using a number 2 plain nozzle, pipe vertical straight lines down the side of the cake in royal icing.
4. Using a basket weave nozzle, pipe horizontal lines over one vertical line and then stop at the next vertical line and begin again at the other side of that line.
5. Using the same nozzle, pipe scallops around the top and the bottom of the cake and allow to set.
6. Decorate with fresh flowers.

Pink Heart Fondant Cake

Serves 8 **Prep time** 45 minutes

Ingredients

2 heart vanilla sponge cakes, 1 medium,
1 small (see page 18)

buttercream icing

200 g / 7 oz / 1 cup apricot jam (jelly)

1 ½ kg / 2 ¾ lbs / 5 cups light pink fondant
icing (see pages 14–15)

few drops of pink food dye

350 g / 12 oz / 1 ¾ cup dark pink fondant
icing (see pages 14–15)

royal icing

50 g / 1 ¾ oz / ¼ cup green fondant icing
(see pages 14–15)

50 g / 1 ¾ oz / ¼ cup white fondant icing
(see pages 14–15)

Method

1. Slice the cakes in half, horizontally. Spread the bottom half with most of
the buttercream and the top half with jam. Sandwich together.
2. Roll out the light pink fondant to cover the cake board. Brush the cake
board with water. Using a rolling pin, lift the fondant and lay it on the board.
3. Use a sharp knife to trim the excess. Cover the 2 heart cakes with the light
pink fondant and allow the fondant to harden.
4. Stack the cakes centrally onto the board. Add pink food dye to the remaining
buttercream and pipe around the base of each tier using a snail trail pattern.
5. Make a fondant wrap for the bottom tier. Roll out two thirds of the dark pink
fondant icing and stamp a border cutter into the icing. Carefully slice along
the bottom.
6. Stick the fondant wrap around the iced board using the royal icing to glue.
7. Stamp out some leaves from the green fondant and create some roses using
the remaining dark pink fondant. Cut out some hearts from the white fondant
and use a ball tool to shape.
8. Stick the roses, leaves and hearts in place using a small amount of royal icing
and allow to set.

103

Peach Wedgewood Celebration Cake

Serves 8 **Prep time** 2 hours

Ingredients

30 cm (12 in) square chocolate sponge cake
(see page 19)

2 kg / 4 lbs 5 oz / 9 cups fondant icing
(see pages 14–15)

peach food dye

300 g / 10 oz / 1 ⅓ cups royal icing
(see page 27)

Method

1. Dye the fondant icing with the food dye, kneading well to achieve a consistent shade.
2. Cover the cake with fondant icing, using a cake smoother to get a smooth, professional finish. Trim away any excess icing.
3. Pipe a line of royal icing down each corner of the cake.
4. Using pins and a piece of string or chain, mark out where you will ice the swags.
5. Pipe over the indentations with royal icing.
6. Pipe a second icing swag underneath each original one. Pipe a bow between and 6 small beads below each swag.
7. Pipe a line of beading around the top the cake. Continue to build up the lines of beading, being careful to keep the lines as straight and uniform as possible.
8. Pipe a line of icing to border the beading. Finally, pipe a joined-up row of beading around the base of the cake where it meets the board.

Ivory Rose Cake

Serves 8 **Prep time** 1 hour

Ingredients

1 heart-shaped vanilla sponge cake
(see page 18)

110 g / 4 oz / ½ cup apricot jam (jelly)

icing (confectioners') sugar to dust

1 kg / 2 lbs 2 oz / 4 ½ cups ivory fondant
icing (see pages 14–15)

Method

1. Brush the top and sides of the cake with apricot jam.
2. Dust the work surface with icing sugar and roll out the icing.
    Use a rolling pin to cover the cake with icing, then mould it down
    and over the sides.
3. Trim away the excess icing and reserve. Use half of the fondant trimmings
    to make the roses. Flatten small balls of the paste between cling film
    to make the petals.
4. Build the roses up, petal by petal, attaching them with a dab of water.
5. Position the roses on top of the cake.
6. Use a pump action sugarcraft gun to extrude a long strip of fondant
    icing, then wrap it around the cake where it meets the board.

Ice Cream Cake

Serves 4 **Prep time** 1 hour

Ingredients

500 ml / 17 fl. oz / 1 pint strawberry
ice cream

300 ml / 10 ½ fl. oz / 1 ¼ cups raspberry
ice cream

300 ml / 10 ½ fl. oz / 1 ¼ cups pistachio
ice cream

300 ml / 10 ½ fl. oz / 1 ¼ cups mango
ice cream

3 brandy snaps

2 tbsp soured cream

redcurrants

Method

1. Preheat the oven to 180ºC (160ºC fan) / 350F / gas 4. Press the strawberry ice cream into the bottom of a 20 cm (8 in) cake mould and freeze.
2. Use a melon baller to shape balls from the other ice creams and make a rose pattern in the surface with a knife.
3. Spread the ice cream balls out on a baking tray and freeze until firm. Spread the brandy snaps out on a baking tray and put them in the oven for 2–3 minutes or until they become pliable.
4. Meanwhile, make a horn shape out of scrunched up foil. When the brandy snaps come out of the oven, mould them around the foil horn and leave to cool and set.
5. Take the ice cream cake out of the freezer and spread the top with soured cream. Place back into the freezer to set.
6. Lay the brandy snap horn on its side and arrange the frozen ice cream balls to the side. Decorate with sprigs of fresh redcurrants.

Ice Cream Macaroon Cake

Serves 6 **Prep time** 30 minutes

Ingredients

20 different macaroons (see page 25)

3 egg whites

150 g / 5 oz / 1 ¼ cup caster (superfine) sugar

½ tsp cornflour (cornstarch)

½ tsp white wine vinegar

20 scoops of ice cream

250 ml / 8 ½ fl. oz / 1 cup double (heavy) cream

redcurrants and raspberries to decorate

Method

1. Preheat the oven to 140ºC (120°C fan) / 240F / gas 2. Line a baking sheet with baking paper and draw on 1 large and 1 medium circle.
2. Whisk the egg whites and half the sugar, then add the remaining sugar and whisk until firm peaks are formed. Fold in the cornflour and vinegar. Spoon the mixture into a piping bag and pipe the meringue onto the baking paper, using the circles as a guide.
3. Bake in the oven for 10 minutes, then turn the oven down to 120°C (100°C fan) / 220F / gas 1 for 45 minutes. Remove the meringues from the oven and allow to cool.
4. Using a melon baller, scoop various ice creams into small balls. Place in the middle of the macaroons and freeze until needed.
5. Once the meringue has cooled, whip the cream and pipe a circle into the centre of the larger circle and place alternating macaroon shells around the edge of the base.
6. Place the medium meringue on top of the bottom layer and add more filled macaroons. Pipe whipped cream onto the top macaroons. Decorate with redcurrants and raspberries.

Chestnut Flan

Serves 6 **Prep time** 15 minutes **Cooking time** 1 hour

Ingredients

500 g / 17 oz / 2 ¼ cups shortcrust pastry

115 g / 4 oz / ½ cup butter, melted

500 g / 17 oz / 2 cups chestnut purée

a pinch of nutmeg

a pinch of salt

4 eggs

2 egg yolks

5 sheets of filo pastry

icing (confectioners') sugar,
    for dusting

8 candied chestnuts

orange zest

1 vanilla pod

edible gold leaf

Method

1. Preheat the oven to 180ºC (160°C fan) / 350F / gas 4.
2. Line a greased flan tin with shortcrust pastry and fill with baking beans. Blind bake for 15 minutes. Remove from the oven, discard the beans and return to the oven for 5 minutes.
3. In a bowl, mix together 100 g of the melted butter with the chestnut purée, nutmeg and salt.
4. In a separate bowl, whisk together the eggs and egg yolks, then combine with the chestnut mix.
5. Pour the mix into pastry case and cook in the oven for 35 minutes until the mixture is firm.
6. Cut the filo pastry into equal-sized squares and brush with melted butter.
7. Lay one sheet on top of another sheet at oblique angles to make a star shape. Scrunch the sheets in the centre to form a flower shape and place in a muffin tin to retain the shape while baking.
8. Place the filo flowers in the oven and remove when crisp and golden. When the flan is cool, dust with icing sugar.
9. Arrange the filo flowers on top. Scatter the candied chestnuts and orange zest around the flowers.
10. Arrange the vanilla pod so that it stands up. Gild the candied chestnuts with the edible gold leaf.

Gold Ribbon Cake

Serves 4–6 **Prep time** 1 hour

Ingredients

round vanilla sponge with white
    fondant icing (see pages 18 and 14–15)

100 g / 3 ½ oz / ½ cup royal icing
    (see page 27)

500 g / 17 oz / 2 cups white fondant icing
    (see pages 14–15)

edible gold leaf

gold ribbons

Method

1. Using a leaf-pattern stencil and flat side scraper tool, scrape the royal icing over the top of the cake and allow to dry.
2. Form a rope by twisting a single length of white fondant and stick in swags around the cake.
3. At the top of each swag, stick a pearl-drop-shaped piece of fondant on the cake.
4. Using a craft knife or small paint brush, apply gold leaf to the pearl drops.
5. Using a leaf nozzle, pipe two royal icing leaf shapes onto the pearl drops and rope swags.
6. Fix ribbon around the base of the cake. Tie a bow in a ribbon and place this on the top of the cake.

White Chocolate Wedding Cake

Serves 10–15 **Prep time** 1 hour 25 minutes

Ingredients

10 cm (4 in) square vanilla sponge with
    fondant icing (see pages 18 and 14–15)

15 cm (6 in) square vanilla sponge with
    fondant icing (see pages 18 and 14–15)

20 cm (8 in) square vanilla sponge with
    fondant icing (see pages 18 and 14–15)

1 kg / 2.2 lbs / 10 cups white chocolate

cream satin ribbon

fresh hydrangeas

florists' wire

2.5 cm (1 in) thick polystyrene blocks

Method

1. Pour half of the melted chocolate onto a marble slab.
2. Using a palette knife, spread the chocolate and allow to cool until almost hard. Score lines in the chocolate, 8 cm (3 in) apart. Push a sharp, slightly oiled blade at a low angle across the chocolate to create long, uniform rolls.
3. Place the cakes on cake boards, each board slightly larger than the cakes. Coat the sides of the cakes in melted chocolate.
4. Stick the chocolate rolls to the sides of all the cakes.
5. Push support dowels into the bottom and middle tiers of the cake.
6. Melt the remaining chocolate as above and use it to stick more chocolate rolls to the boards of the cake. When set, surround the cake boards with cream satin ribbon.
7. Trim the hydrangea stems and insert short lengths of wire into the stems, leaving about 3 cm (1 in) of wire sticking out of the end of each blossom.
8. Place a polystyrene block on the top of the bottom tier, ensuring it rests on the dowels.
9. Push the wired hydrangeas into the polystyrene around the cake tier. Place the second tier of cake onto the polystyrene block and repeat the last stage. Put the final tier of cake in place and top with hydrangeas to complete the cake.

Chocolate and Cream Wedding Cake

Serves 60 **Prep time** 3 hours

Ingredients

40 cm (16 in) round vanilla sponge cake
(see page 18)

20 cm (8 in) round vanilla sponge cake (see
page 18)

15 cm (6 in) round vanilla sponge cake (see
page 18)

40 cm (16 in) round chocolate sponge cake
(see page 19)

20 cm (8 in) round chocolate sponge cake
(see page 19)

15 cm (6 in) round chocolate sponge cake
(see page 19)

225g / 8 oz / 1 cup unsalted butter,
softened

a few drops of vanilla extract

450g / 1 lb / 3 ½ cups icing (confectioners')
sugar

2–3 tbsp milk

3 kg / 6 lbs 8 oz / 13 cups fondant icing
(see pages 14–15)

brown food dye

600 g / 1 lb 5 oz / 2 ½ cups royal icing
(see page 27)

sugared almonds

sugar pearls

silver sugar balls

Method

1. To make the buttercream, beat the butter in a large mixing bowl until smooth; add the vanilla extract and half of the icing sugar.
2. Stir briefly to incorporate before beating with an electric whisk until thick and pale.
3. Add the remaining icing sugar and some of the milk; continue to beat until very pale and smooth.
4. Split the larger vanilla sponge horizontally into three pieces; stack two on either side of the large chocolate sponge.
5. Spread the top of the stacked sponges with a third of the buttercream; sit the third round of vanilla sponge on top of the buttercream, then cover the tops and sides with a thin layer of buttercream.
6. Repeat for the two smaller cakes.
7. Dye the fondant icing with the brown food dye, kneading well to remove any streaks.
8. Roll out the fondant icing and use it to cover each cake, using a cake smoother to get a smooth, professional finish. Trim away any excess icing. Stack the cakes on top of each other, securing with a little royal icing.
9. Use a pastry cutter to gently mark the edges of the cake as a guide for the royal icing.
10. Using the indentations as a guide, use the royal icing to pipe swags around the cake. Pipe beads of royal icing between the swags.
11. Attach the sugared almonds, pearls and sugar balls to the cake with a little royal icing.
12. Use a piping bag fitted with a star nozzle to pipe a row of shell beading where the cakes meet.

Peach Wedding Cake

Serves 10 **Prep time** 1 hour 25 minutes

Ingredients

3 circular vanilla sponge cakes in increasing sizes 15 cm, 20 cm, 25 cm (6 in, 8 in and 10 in) (see page 18)

500 g /1 lb 3 oz / 2 ¼ cups buttercream

2 kg / 4 ½ lbs / 10 cups white fondant icing (see page 14–15)

icing (confectioners') sugar (optional)

15 cm (6 in) round vanilla sponge (see page 18)

20 cm (8 in) round vanilla sponge (see page 18)

25 cm (10 in) round vanilla sponge (see page 18)

edible glue

200 g / 7oz / 2 cups royal icing (see page 27)

peach food dye

Method

1. Cover the sponges with buttercream, then cover with rolled white fondant and trim away any excess.
2. Use a cake smoother to smooth out any blemishes. Use a little icing sugar if the fondant sticks.
3. Draw scroll patterns onto baking paper. Place the template against the cake. Using a scribing tool, carefully mark out the pattern you wish to pipe onto the surface.
4. Dye some fondant with peach food dye and roll into a 3 mm ($^1/_8$ in) thick sheet. Cut a strip about 1.5 cm (½ in) wide and about 12 cm (5 in) long.
5. Lay a clean pen about a third of the way in from each end of the fondant. Roll the fondant back over the pens until they ends meet to create a bow shape. Seal the ends down with edible glue.
6. Take a shorter strip about 3 cm (1 in) long and wrap this around the middle of the bow to make a loop, then stick down with edible glue. Make 12–15 loops and set aside to harden.
7. Make between 22–24 loops and leave to one side.
8. Pipe beads around the bottom of the cake where it meets the board. Repeat this around each cake tier.
9. Adhere 14–16 of the prepared bows on top of the cake, sticking them down with edible glue.
10. Stick the remaining bows to the sides of the tiers of the cake; roll out any remaining dye before cutting into 16 strips approximately 8–10 cm (3–4 in) x 2–3 cm (1–2 in) wide.
11. Use some edible glue to stick the strips of fondant underneath the bows on the side of the cake so that they drape and fold at the bottom; leave to dry and harden before serving the cake.

Yellow Ribbon and Roses Birthday Cake

Serves 25 **Prep time** 3 hours (plus 24 hours for setting)

Ingredients

30 cm (12 in) round vanilla sponge cake (see page 18)

23 cm (9 in) round vanilla sponge cake (see page 18)

15 cm (6 in) round chocolate sponge cake (see page 19)

2.5 kg / 5 ½ lbs / 11 cups yellow fondant icing (pages 14–15)

300 g / 10 oz / 1 ⅓ cups royal icing (see page 27)

200 g / 7 oz / ¾ cup sugar florist paste

green food dye

edible lustre (optional)

500 g / 1 lb 1 oz / 2 ½ cups isomalt

55 g / 2 oz / 3 tbsp liquid glucose

pink food dye

Method

1. Cover each cake with yellow fondant icing, using a cake smoother to get a smooth finish. Trim away any excess icing. Stack the cakes on top of each other, securing with royal icing.
2. Use a pump action sugarcraft gun to extrude a long strip of fondant icing. Fold the strip in half and twist to form a rope.
3. Draw a lace pattern onto tracing paper and transfer the design to the side of the cake by pricking through the paper. Use white royal icing to pipe over the design.
4. Use the fondant rope to hide the join between the cakes, securing with a little royal icing.
5. To make the rose petals, flatten out small balls of florist paste between your fingers, then thin the petals using a ball tool and a foam pad.
6. Assemble the roses using water or flower glue to attach the petals to each other. Leave roses to harden for 24 hours before brushing with edible lustre.
7. Dye the remaining sugar paste with a little green food dye. Roll it out as thin as possible and use a rose leaf cutter to cut out the leaves. Dust with edible lustre and leave to harden for 24 hours over scrunched foil to give a natural shape.
8. To make the ribbons, stir the isomalt over a low heat until the crystals dissolve. Add the glucose and boil. Add a little pink food dye, then pour onto an oiled marble slab to cool. Put small pieces of the cooled isomalt under a heat lamp. When pliable, pull each piece until thin.
9. Bend the sugar ribbon round into a loop. Pinch away any excess paste and repeat to form the rest of the ribbon loops. Assemble the pulled sugar ribbons on top of the cake, and decorate the lower tiers with the roses and leaves.

Rings and Flowers Cake

Serves 10–15 **Prep time** 1 hour

Ingredients

2 large vanilla sponge cakes (see page 18)

375 g / 12 oz / 1 cup buttercream

500 g / 1 lb 3 oz / 2 ¼ cups royal icing (see page 27)

1 large bar white chocolate

250 g / 8 oz / 1 ½ cups of white fondant icing (see pages 14–15)

red food dye

yellow food dye

green food dye

Method

1. Cover the sponges with a thin layer of buttercream and then spread with the royal icing.
2. Make shavings of white chocolate by using a sharp knife and pressing down on the edge of the chocolate bar.
3. Sprinkle the cakes with white chocolate.
4. Dye small amounts of fondant with red, yellow and green food dye. Roll the red and green fondants into 3 mm (¹/₈ in) thick sheets. Cut out circles of red fondant and roll them in your fingers to form rose centres.
5. Using a leaf-shaped cutter, cut out leaves from the green fondant. Roll the yellow fondant into a long sausage shape with a cake smoother, then cut and form two rings and interlink them.
6. Allow all the fondant to harden. Arrange the roses, rings and leaves on the cakes, place on doilies or cake boards and serve.

INDEX